AF

Judith Shea

Lynda Forsha

La Jolla Museum of
Contemporary Art

La Jolla Museum of
Contemporary Art
March 18 - May 22, 1988

University Gallery
University of Massachusetts,
Amherst
October 28 - December 14, 1988

This exhibition was made
possible by the generous
contributions of
Dr. Ivor Royston and
Colette Carson Royston
and the Corporate Benefactors,
a group of business
and professional leaders who
provide important financial
support to the Museum.

The exhibition is part of the
Museum's Parameters series,
funded in part by the National
Endowment for the Arts, a
federal agency.

Library of Congress Catalogue Card Number
88-080194
ISBN 0-934418-29-2

Cover:
Bop, 1980, rayon taffeta
36" x 27" x 1 1/2"

PREFACE

Judith Shea emerged as a sculptor of substantial power when her witty and enigmatic dress works were included in the Whitney Biennial of 1981. These bas-couture garments, minimal uniforms redolent of fifties form, seemed the quintessential sculptural counterpart of the New Image painting of Robert Moskowitz and Susan Rothenberg. Though painting has dominated exhibitions generally over the past decade, sculpture, such as Shea's, has flourished undaunted.

In their softness and everyday reference, Shea's first fabric pieces recalled Claes Oldenburg's padded pop objects slimmed down for the minimal sixties. But subsequent works revealed a more abiding link with a figurative tradition reaching back to Rome, Greece, Egypt, and Mesopotamia. The clothes evoked, if not made, the man and woman. The cloth works seem contemporary counterparts to the compelling, anonymous draped figures of the Pergamon Altar. More recent cast metal pieces variously recall medieval knights in armor and repose, Far Eastern divinities memorialized in temples and shrines, and the more abstract biomorphic forms of Brancusi and Arp. While Shea has an undeniably strong formal vocabulary and a solid grounding in the history of her medium, in the final analysis it is her overriding humanistic instincts and powerful abilities of observation which distinguish the sculpture and mark her impressive achievement.

In presenting this exhibition, we are first and foremost indebted to Judith Shea, who has been unwaveringly generous with her time and thoughts as this exhibition has been assembled. Curator Lynda Forsha has for many years had a strong affinity for Shea's work. Here her curatorial talents have dovetailed perfectly with Shea's art and the success of their collaboration is evidenced in the selection of works and the illuminating essay included in this publication. While Shea's sculpture like all great art eludes categorization, this exhibition serves to bring her impressive achievement into clearer focus.

Hugh M. Davies
Director

Holding It In, 1983
cast iron
15″ x 9″ x 3 1/2″
Collection of Chase Manhattan Bank,
New York City

ACKNOWLEDGMENTS

The Dobe, 1980
cotton chintz, wooden dowel
29 1/2″ x 36″ x 1/2″

Assembling an exhibition necessarily involves the cooperation of many individuals and institutions. Curt Marcus and Gordon VeneKlasen of the Curt Marcus Gallery have been helpful in all steps of the preparation of the exhibition and catalogue. Julie Dunn's editorial guidance was crucial to the catalogue's completion. We are grateful for the care Craig Fuller has shown in the design of the catalogue, meticulously assembled by Jennifer Leich. On our staff, Mary Hylaman and Victoria Reed compiled the biography and bibliography with exacting detail. Bolton Colburn, Mary Johnson, and Marilyn Mannisto coordinated the loans for the work in the exhibition, while David Jurist prepared the final installation. Special thanks to Janet Ciaffone, Anne Farrell, Madeleine Grynsztejn, Norman Hannay, Gloria Jung, and Diane Maxwell for their support of this project.

Additionally, we are grateful to the individuals and institutions who so graciously loaned us their work, especially since the exhibition is traveling after its La Jolla premiere. We thank the Edward R. Broida Trust, the Brooklyn Museum, the Chase Manhattan Bank, Linda and Ronald F. Daitz, Dart Gallery, Charles Harrison and Linda Rawson, Ellis and Ellen Kern, Miani Johnson, Raymond J. Learsy, Curt Marcus Gallery, and the Neuberger Museum. Our gratitude also extends to Helaine Posner at the University Gallery, University of Massachusetts, Amherst for joining us in hosting the exhibition.

The project would not have been possible without the generous contributions of Dr. Ivor Royston and Colette Carson Royston, and the Museum's business and professional patrons, the Corporate Benefactors. In addition, the project was part of the Museum's Parameters series, funded by the National Endowment for the Arts, a federal agency.

I would especially like to thank Hugh Davies, Ron Onorato, and Craig Fuller for their interest and support of this project, and for their editorial guidance on the essay in this catalogue.

Finally, I would like to extend my heartfelt appreciation to Judith for her care, patience, good humor, and insightfulness during the preparation of the exhibition and this publication.

LF

Spin Trinity, 1985
bronze
12 1/2″ x 14″ x 19 1/2″

Installation view of Shea works included in the
Seven Artists exhibition at the Neuberger
Museum, State University of New York at
Purchase, 1981. (left to right) *Exec. Sec'y.* 1980,
5 pm 1980, *Photoplay* 1980, and *Posture* 1980.

JUDITH SHEA

Lynda Forsha

The work of Judith Shea occupies a unique niche in the realm of significant sculpture. With the resurgence of figurative art in the mid-seventies, Shea's work alone is defined by an investigation of clothing — clothing both as sculptural object and as surrogate for human form.

As is apparent from her work, Shea's fascination with articles of dress is finely honed, and the resulting works of art are elegant and archetypal in form and in purpose. This is clothing that sheathes the body and derives sculpturally from the figure in a manner that is timeless and free of the cosmetic extravagance of fashion or ornamentation.

Shea's formal strategy is a synthesis of the minimalist conception of "essential form" combined with the fluid and organic nature of cloth. The subtle, compound masses that clothing delineates when draped or wrapped about the human body are sculpturally reviewed through the legacy of reductivist abstraction. Her work has evolved during the past decade from wall hangings—nearly flat, graphic silhouettes concerned almost entirely with their rectilinear construction—to the most recent free-standing pieces which combine formal and iconographic strategies that seek to reconcile reductivist and classical notions of form and beauty.

Obsessed with dressmaking and design from an early age, Shea attended Parsons School of Design with the idea of becoming a fashion designer. However, by the late sixties, fashion had abandoned strict structural concerns in favor of more cosmetic issues. To her additional dismay, she discovered through subsequent job experience that designers rarely enjoyed the kind of hands-on process of constructing a garment.[1]

Seeing the promise of the fashion industry fade, she returned to Parsons to study art and received her B.F.A. in 1975. Through a summer residency at Artpark in 1974, Shea became clearly aware of her kinship with other artists who were similarly interested in investigating structural issues, and began to clarify her own stake in the aesthetic and conceptual milieu of that time.

Shea's first widely exhibited works date from the mid-seventies following the Artpark summer. These "clothing constructions" consist of fabric sections sewn together to create the appearance of various articles of clothing. The individual works are installed flat against the wall, and hung primarily from a single horizontal dowel. This two-dimensional silhouette evokes the paper templates of pattern pieces prior to construction. (A shirt, for instance, might be divided into front-and-back, left-and-right panels, along with adjoining collars or sleeves. An abstracted inventory of a garment, itself an abstracted variant of the body part it serves to cover.)

Shea began the development of each "construction" with the fabric, considering its physical and associative qualities, and allowing

New Man, 1986
bronze
26″ x 16″ x 12″

7

shape and character to lead her to an image of the type of garment that would best elaborate the particular quality of the material.

As very shallow wall works (bas-reliefs) these pieces equivocate between painting and sculpture. At once "shaped-canvases" and objects of literal, quasi-functional import, they play off both the aesthetics of two-dimensional abstraction and the sculptural potential of "occupied" garments.

Additionally, these cloth sculptures serve to bridge the gap between art and craft/design. While fabric, specifically canvas, is the normal ground for mainstream painting, cloth as pure material ironically has endured the tainted status of a "craft" medium. Yet Shea's quality of intention catapults this work well beyond the "handsome object" mentality of much crafts-related work.

Though works from this period all share a clear constructivist orientation, it is not entirely at the expense of referential imagery. With great economy of means, Shea has managed to evoke a surprising variety of historic and cultural moments from pop clothing in *Bop, I Like Ike*, and *The Dobe*, to haute couture in *Inaugural Ball*, all 1980.

Alternately sardonic and sympathetic, these references generate a level of content wholly beyond the dispassionate purity of doctrinaire minimalism. If the minimalist's vision of the sublime was an ascetic one, Shea's early work develops a more synthetic and ultimately figurative vision, which is no less grounded in the Aristotelian notion of "universal form" than that of the minimalists.

3 Square Shirts, 1977, which was made at the Fabric Workshop in Philadelphia, exhibits the juxtaposition of geometrically printed fabric with that of clothing construction. White yardage is printed in solid primary colors that occupy the square dimensions of the interior of the silk-screen frame. These colored squares abut, forming crisp edges between one color region and another, while occasionally and quite deliberately, the white, unprinted fabric appears as a narrow strip between or around the color masses. The fabric is cut into four pieces for each "construction." The pieces for the torso, collar, and armpit gusset are square, hence the title of the work. The piece for the sleeve is rectangular. Combined, the four pieces form a vertical "peasant" shirt which appears to have been folded back upon itself longitudinally. In presenting five color pattern combinations from a series and system that potentially extends to dozens of permutations, Shea suggests the range of possibilities for combining color structure and shirt construction. The systematic combination of elementary geometric form and primary color extends a rigorous modernist tradition that includes such artists as Piet Mondrian to Ellsworth Kelly and Sol Lewitt. Yet these brilliant fabric pieces even more vividly evoke the

I Like Ike, 1980
canvas
44″ x 19″ x 2″
Collection of Miani Johnson,
New York City

3 Square Shirts, 1977
silk–screened cotton, wooden dowel
22 1/2″ x 36″ x 1/2″ each
Printed at the Fabric Workshop, Inc.

Studio view of *Checked Pants* and
other works in progress.
Checked Pants, 1977-78
wire mesh
42″ x 20″ x 10″

chromatic geometry of flags, specifically the colorful vocabulary of nautical signal pennants.

During the late seventies, Shea embarked on a series of wholly three-dimensional pieces made with wire mesh and sheet metal. While these works foreshadow the fully volumetric cast pieces of the eighties, Shea concluded that in constructing with sheet metal she was unable to mimic the suppleness of cloth and, ultimately, the dynamic subtlety of human gesture.

In *Checked Pants*, 1977-78, cloth-like undulations are achieved through the manipulation of gridded wire mesh, a pliable yet rigid material. The grid becomes a topological map of the uneven surface contour, while the transparent properties of the mesh material permit a simultaneous and superimposed pant reading front and back - inside and outside. The whimsical title loads the gridded mesh with yet another message — the reminder of the actual woven pattern of the imagined fabric. A wonderful irony emerges between the rigorous reference to the Agnes Martin/Sol Lewitt minimal grid and the vernacular association of plaid fabric never missing from the links.

By 1980, Shea began using heavier materials, industrial felt, cast iron, etc., and her wall constructions became less flacid, more volumetric. Some pieces employ garment construction techniques such as gathered folds, darts, and pleats to cause the front face of the "garment" to emerge from the wall. Dark, often monochromatic color strategies tend to reinforce a more starkly sculptural reading of these pieces. Through the specific identity of each piece, the issue of gender becomes clearer, with curves and protrusions characterizing female apparel, and rectilinear contours defining more masculine tailoring. The dowels, once an invisible support element, are now used as a deliberate formal element to create a linear counterpoint to the mass of the clothing shape, and to echo the contour of the top edge of the "garment" by extending its curve or angle. Like *Checked Pants*, these works are often titled to emphasize cultural associations that belie their rather severe formal presence.

B-Vest, 1981, exemplifies the somber and more sculptural nature of this period. It was designed in partnership and in counterpoint to *Ahab*, 1981. Both works are half-pieces of clothing made from dark felt with the natural color of the felt on one side and colored felt (silk-screened) on the inside. While *Ahab*'s references are masculine—a trouser leg, phallic-shaped, alone and defiant both in title and posture—*B-Vest* registers a calmer and more covert attitude. Formally it is composed of a series of arched contours that in silhouette and relief delineate the female torso. The volume of its front panel is formed by the dart that also reads as the lone and poignant figure on an otherwise solid and continuous surface. The ochre "facade" largely

O Kazimir, 1981
felt, paint, chalk, wooden dowel
22" x 24" x 1/2"

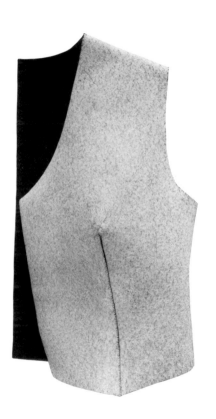

B-Vest, 1981
felt with textile paint
20″ x 15″ x 3″

conceals and protects the dark, concave interior form of the piece which underscores *B-Vest*'s brooding, impassive countenance. The name *B-Vest*, in typical Shea fashion, counters the mood of the piece by referencing the yellow and black coloration of a bumble bee.

While these constructions enjoy stronger sculptural characteristics than the earlier hanging work, the softness of the fabric placed limitations on Shea's ability to investigate increasingly volumetric forms, clothing filled-out and enlivened by the human occupant.

In 1981, while teaching a class in Medieval European Armor at the Metropolitan Museum of Art in New York, Shea gained a working knowledge of early battle armor. Most armor on public exhibition is ceremonial, originally worn by royalty and high-ranking officers, and consequently adorned with ornamental embellishments. But the armor that Shea discovered was modest, straightforward, and above all, made for protection and mobility. Through these objects Shea began to see the possibility that cast metal would have as a rigid material with which to more fully investigate shape and gesture in three-dimensional space.

In 1982, Shea produced *Crusader*, one of her first cast pieces. As with those that followed, she began the work by constructing the form of the piece out of the same heavy industrial felts that had already been used. But now a mold was built around the felt form and molten iron was poured into it, burning away the felt and cooling in its place. Just as Shea's articles of clothing were beginning to stand for human form, so would the cast metal become a surrogate material for the original felt and wax model.

In *Crusader* one sees cast metal replicating the hammered metal and chain mail used in medieval armor. Here, Shea has ingeniously employed the longitudinal half-fragments of clothing to depict a slain soldier sunk into the mire of the battlefield. Though it is not significantly more complex in form than some of her earlier works, *Crusader* clearly references the figure and the human event *within* the "wrapper" of the clothing and, in so doing, the work announces not only a more volumetric means but, most importantly, a clearly assertive depiction of content in Shea's work.

Through the use of patina, which can be produced with the application of chemicals, Shea is able to give ancient and archaeological qualities to her cast work, qualities that reaffirm the rather timeless and archetypal reading of the forms themselves, placing their depiction into a removed historical context. This ability allowed Shea to pursue her long-standing interest in history in general. It also provided a powerful tool in her continued movement away from nonreferential construction towards a more personal, synthetic vision that could now

Black Dress, 1983
wool felt, India ink, and wax
44 1/2″ x 15″ x 12″
Collection of Raymond J. Learsy,
New York City
(included only in La Jolla Museum exhibition)

The work of the mid–eighties, all fully volumetric, tends to play pure geometric elements against figurative form. In some pieces— *Black Dress*, 1983, or *Good Girl*, 1985—the base both mimics and counters the form of the supported figure above. In others, such as *New Man* and *The Balance*, both 1986, the geometric volume interacts with the figure in a more specially metaphorical if open-ended manner.

As her work has evolved, gradually moving from purely syntactic to more semantic concerns, Shea has reconsidered the formal and historical significance of various periods constituting the vast tradition of figurative sculpture. While her recent pieces evoke a diversity of classical Greek, Oriental and medieval sources, all fit neatly within the spare formal elegance of the "classical" tradition.

To push her exploration one step further, Shea has more recently engaged in extracting new meaning from both the rather extravagant style of 19th-century European sculpture as well as ancient Egyptian statuary.

The Balance in particular elicits a wealth of interpretive possibilities of the relationship of the diminutive cube to the ancient robed, sage-like figure. Could this be the Greek mathematician Euclid, father of geometry, contemplating his offspring? Or perhaps it is a variation of the virgin and child tableaux with geometry achieving divine status? Shea more likely thought in terms of representing two traditions, that of classicism/figuration in relation to cubist driven modernism, and suggests here that the latter is necessarily the rather young offspring of the former — different, perhaps in formal strategy, but genetically linked, nonetheless.

It is this very connection of abstract and representational traditions that has always been at the contemplative heart of Shea's work. With clothing as her guide and catalyst, Shea has navigated in a dozen short years from the relative straightjacket of minimalism to a body of recent work that, in its richness and breadth of meaning, has established Shea as a true heir to sculpture's most ancient and durable tradition.

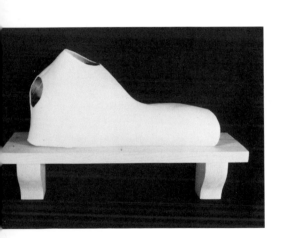

Shelf Piece, 1983
wool, felt, wax
13″ x 26″ x 11″
Collection of General Mills Corporation,
Minneapolis, Minnesota

NOTES

Information throughout this essay has been drawn from conversations with the artist in New York City on April 30, September 23 and September 25, 1987.

[1]Helen Raye, "Judith Shea." In *Structure to Resemblance - Work by Eight American Sculptors*, (Albright-Knox Art Gallery, 1987), p.45.

[2]Wade Saunders, "Talking Objects: Interviews with Ten Younger Sculptors," *Art in America*, vol. 73, no. 11 (November 1985), p. 119.

The Balance, 1986
bronze and birchwood
36 1/2″ x 28 1/2″ x 21″

Collection of the Brooklyn Museum,
Ira and Wendy Weinstein and Carll H.
DeSilver Fund,
Brooklyn, New York

Eden, 1987
bronze
65″ x 35″ x 18 1/2″

EXHIBITION CHECKLIST

Height precedes width, width precedes depth.

3 Square Shirts, 1977
silk-screened cotton, wooden dowel
22 1/2" x 36" x 1/2" each
Printed at the Fabric Workshop, Inc.
Courtesy of Curt Marcus Gallery,
New York City

Checked Pants, 1977-78
wire mesh
42" x 20" x 10"
Courtesy of Curt Marcus Gallery,
New York City

Bop, 1980
rayon taffeta
36" x 27" x 1 1/2"
Courtesy of Curt Marcus Gallery,
New York City

I Like Ike, 1980
canvas
44" x 19" x 2"
Collection of Miani Johnson,
New York City

Nylons, 1980
silk organza (4 parts)
34" x 7" each
Collection of Neuberger Museum,
State University of New York at
Purchase, Gift of Martin J. Sklar,
Purchase, New York

Tank, 1980
cotton organdy
25 3/4" x 14 1/2"
Collection of Miani Johnson,
New York City

The Dobe, 1980
cotton chintz, wooden dowel
29 1/2" x 36" x 1/2"
Courtesy of Curt Marcus Gallery,
New York City

Ahab, 1981
felt with textile paint
40" x 9" x 8"
Collection of Charles Harrison and
Linda Rawson,
New York City

B-Vest, 1981
felt with textile paint
20" x 15" x 3"
Courtesy of Curt Marcus Gallery,
New York City

O Kazimir, 1981
felt, paint, chalk, wooden dowel
22" x 24" x 1/2"
Courtesy of Curt Marcus Gallery,
New York City

Sling, 1981
textile paint on canvas
16" x 10" x 4"
Collection of Ellis and Ellen Kern,
New York City

Crusader, 1982
cast iron
2 parts T. 16" x 9" x 5"
       B. 21" x 15 1/2" x 4"
Courtesy of Dart Gallery,
Chicago, Illinois

Black Dress, 1983
wool felt, India ink, and wax
44 1/2" x 15" x 12"
Collection of Raymond J. Learsy,
New York City
(included only in La Jolla Museum
exhibition)

Crawl, 1983
bronze
22" x 11 1/2" x 6"
Collection of the Edward R. Broida
Trust,
Los Angeles, California

Holding It In, 1983
cast iron
15" x 9" x 3 1/2"
Collection of Chase Manhattan Bank,
New York City

Shelf Piece, 1983
wool, felt, wax
13" x 26" x 11"
Collection of General Mills Corporation,
Minneapolis, Minnesota

Good Girl, 1985
bronze
53" x 14" x 11"
Collection of Linda and Ronald F. Daitz,
New York City

Spin Trinity, 1985
bronze
12 1/2" x 14" x 19 1/2"
Courtesy of Curt Marcus Gallery,
New York City

New Man, 1986
bronze
26" x 16" x 12"
Courtesy of Curt Marcus Gallery,
New York City

The Balance, 1986
bronze and birchwood
36 1/2" x 28 1/2" x 21"
Collection of the Brooklyn Museum,
Ira and Wendy Weinstein and Carll H.
DeSilver Fund,
Brooklyn, New York

Eden, 1987
bronze
65" x 35" x 18 1/2"
Courtesy of Curt Marcus Gallery,
New York City

Endless Model, 1988
cast stone
7' x 14" x 14"
Courtesy of Curt Marcus Gallery,
New York City

Crawl, 1983
bronze
22″ x 11 1/2″ x 6″
Collection of the Edward R. Broida Trust,
Los Angeles, California

BIOGRAPHY

Born in Philadelphia, Pennsylvania, 1948
Lives and works in New York City

Education

Parsons School of Design, New York City, A.A. Fashion Design, 1969

Parsons School of Design/The New School for Social Research, New York City, B.F.A., 1975

One-Person Exhibitions:

1988   *Judith Shea*, La Jolla Museum of Contemporary Art, La Jolla, California

      Curt Marcus Gallery, New York City

1986   Willard Gallery, New York City

      Judith Shea, New Sculptures, Pennsylvania Academy of Fine Arts, Philadelphia, Pennsylvania

1985   Knight Gallery, Charlotte, North Carolina

1984   Willard Gallery, New York City

1983   Dart Gallery, Chicago, Illinois

      Willard Gallery, New York City

1981   Willard Gallery, New York City

      Judith Shea, Sculpture as Clothing, Washington Square East Galleries, New York City

1980   Willard Gallery, New York City

1978   481, The Women's Center Gallery, New Haven, Connecticut

1976   *Studio Project*, The Clocktower, New York City

Selected Group Exhibitions:

1987   *Sculpture to Resemblance: Work by Eight American Sculptors*, Albright-Knox Art Gallery, Buffalo, New York

      Sculptures on Paper: New Work, Madison Art Center, Madison, Wisconsin

      Bronze, Plaster and Polyester, Moore College of Art Gallery, Philadelphia, Pennsylvania

      The Allusive Object, Barbara Krakow Gallery, Boston, Massachusetts

      Standing Ground: Sculpture by American Women, Contemporary Art Center, Cincinnati, Ohio

1986   *Drawings*, Barbara Krakow Gallery, Boston, Massachusetts

      Contemporary Cutouts, Whitney Museum of American Art, New York City

      Willard Gallery, New York City

      Works on Paper, Althea Viafora Gallery, New York City

      50th Anniversary Exhibition, Willard Gallery, New York City

      Painting and Sculpture Today: 1986, Indianapolis Museum of Art, Indianapolis, Indiana

      Special Project Room, P.S.1 (Institute for Art and Urban Resources), Long Island City, New York

1985   *Body and Soul: Aspects of Recent Figurative Sculpture*, Contemporary Art Center, Cincinnati, Ohio

      Judith Shea/Robert Moskowitz, Hayden Gallery, Massachusetts Institute of Technology, Cambridge, Massachusetts

      Affiliations: Recent Sculpture and Its Antecedents, Whitney Museum at Stamford, Stamford, Connecticut

      In Three Dimensions, Pratt Institute Galleries, New York City

1984   *Currents 4: Art and Use*, Milwaukee Art Museum, Milwaukee, Wisconsin

      Four Sculptors: Ritual and Artifact, Zabriskie Gallery, New York City

      American Sculpture, Margo Leavin Gallery, Los Angeles, California

      Artist in the Theatre, Hillwood Art Gallery, C. W. Post Center, Long Island University, Greenvale, New York

      Judith Shea/Nick Vaughn, Walker Art Center, Minneapolis, Minnesota

1983   *Sculpture Now*, Virginia Museum of Fine Arts, Richmond Virginia

      Artist/Critic, White Columns, New York City

      The New Sculpture, Martina Hamilton Gallery, New York City

      The Sixth Day, Bergman Gallery, The Renaissance Society, University of Chicago, Chicago, Illinois

      Day In/Day Out: Ordinary Life as a Source of Art, Freedman Gallery, Albright College, Reading, Pennsylvania

      Directions 1983, Hirshhorn Museum and Sculpture Garden, Washington, D.C.

      1984 - A Preview, Ronald Feldman Fine Arts, New York City

1982   *Energism*, Arthur Roger Gallery, New Orleans, Louisiana

      Painting and Sculpture Today 1982, Indianapolis Art Expo, Stockholm, Sweden

      Willard Gallery, Stockholm International Art Expo, Stockholm, Sweden

      View by Women Artists; Polychromed Sculpture, Lever House, New York City

      By the Sea, Barbara Toll Fine Arts, New York City

      Willard Gallery, New York City

1981-1984   *Art Materialized, Selections from the Fabric Workshop*, The New Gallery for Contemporary Art, Cincinnati, Ohio
also: Pensacola Museum of Art, Pensacola, Florida; Alberta College Art Gallery, Calgary, Alberta, Canada; University of South Florida Art Galleries, Tampa, Florida; The Hudson River Museum, Yonkers, New York; Gibbs Art Gallery, Charleston, South Carolina

1981   *Parafunction*, Barbara Gladstone Gallery, New York City

      Figuratively Sculpting, P.S.1 (Institute for Art and Urban Resources), Long Island City, New York

      Willard Gallery, *Art 12'81: Swiss Industries Fair*, Basel, Switzerland

      The Soft Land/Il Soffice Paese, Palazzo Farnese, Ortona, Italy

Transformations: Women in Art 70's - 80's, New York Coliseum, New York City

Summer Pleasures, Barbara Gladstone Gallery, New York City

1981 Biennial Exhibition, Whitney Museum of American Art, New York City

1980 Audrey Strohl Gallery, Memphis, Tennessee

Regalia, Henry Street Settlement, New York City

Seven Artists, Neuberger Museum, State University of New York at Purchase, New York

Fabric into Art, Amelie A. Wallace Gallery, State University of New York College at Old Westbury, New York

1979-
1980 *Material Pleasures*, Institute of Contemporary Art, Philadelphia, Pennsylvania; Museum of Contemporary Art, Chicago, Illinois

1979 Marian Locks Gallery, Philadelphia, Pennsylvania

Summertime, Droll/Kobert Gallery, New York City

Clothing Constructions, Los Angeles Institute of Contemporary Art, Los Angeles, California

1978 William Patterson College, Wayne, New Jersey

Willard Gallery, New York City

1977 *Collection in Progress*, Moore College of Art Gallery, Philadelphia, Pennsylvania

1976 *The Handwrought Object*, 1776-1976, Herbert F. Johnson Museum of Art, Cornell University, Ithaca, New York

Rooms, P.S.1 (Institute for Art and Urban Resources), Long Island City, New York

Miami Beach Festival of the Arts, Miami, Florida

1975 Artpark, Lewiston, New York

1974 Artpark, Lewiston, New York

1988 Forsha, Lynda. *Judith Shea.* Exhibition catalogue. La Jolla, California: La Jolla Museum of Contemporary Art.

1987 Gill, Susan. "Judith Shea, Willard." *Art News* (January): 161,163.

Structure to Resemblance: Work by Eight American Sculptors. Exhibition catalogue. Buffalo, New York: Albright-Knox Art Gallery.

Van Wagner, J.C. "Judith Shea: A Personal Balance." *Arts Magazine* (January): 76-77.

1986 *Contemporary Cutouts.* Exhibition catalogue. New York: Whitney Museum of American Art.

1985 *Body and Soul: Recent Figurative Sculpture.* Cincinnati, Ohio: Contemporary Arts Center.

Cohen, Ronny. "Reviews: Judith Shea." *Artforum* (February): 84-85.

Gill, Susan. "New York Reviews: Costumes." *Art News* (April): 149.

Princenthal, Nancy. "Judith Shea, Willard." *Art News* (February): 141,143.

Saunders, Wade. "Talking Objects: Interviews with Ten Sculptors." *Art in America* (November): 110-37.

Taylor, Robert. "Images Endowed with Layers of Meaning at M.I.T." *Boston Globe.*

Westfall, Stephen. "Judith Shea at Willard." *Art in America* (March): 158.

1984 Goldwater, Marge. *Judith Shea/ Nick Vaughn.* Exhibition brochure. Minneapolis, Minnesota: Walker Art Center.

Harris, Susan. "Four Sculptors: Ritual and Artifact." *Arts Magazine* (November): 41-42.

1983 Bernard, April. "Vanity Fair Notes." *Vanity Fair* (May): 24,26.

Cohen, Ronny H. and Peggy Cyphers. "The First Energist Book." *New Observations 9,* March 9.

Directions 1983. Exhibition catalogue. Washington, D.C.: Hirshhorn Museum and Sculpture Garden, Smithsonian Institution.

Gessner, Liz. "Apparel Art." *Gentleman's Quarterly* (May).

Glatt, Cara. "Sculptors Look at Human Form." *The Herald*, May 25, 10.

Koplos, J. "Garment Form as Image." *Fiberarts* (November/December): 69.

Liebmann, Lisa. "Judith Shea." *Artforum* (September): 70.

Levin, Kim. "Top Forms." *The Village Voice*, May 24, 84-85.

Lichtenstein, Therese. "Group Show." *Arts Magazine* (November): 40.

Moser, Charlotte. "Renaissance Show Surveys Ten Years of Using Human Form in Sculpture." *New York Times*, May 29.

Peacock, Mary. "V." *The Village Voice*, February 1, 35.

Sculpture Now. Exhibition catalogue. Richmond, Virginia: Virginia Museum of Fine Art.

Stein, Judith. "The Artist's New Clothes." *Portofolio* (January/February): 63-66.

1982 Siegel, Jeanne. "Figuratively Sculpting P.S.1 (Long Island)." *Art Express* (March).

Van Wagner, Judith K. "Judith Shea: Willard Gallery." *Art Press* (March).

1981 *Art Materialized, Selections from the Fabric Workshop.* Exhibition catalogue. Cleveland, Ohio: The New Gallery for Contemporary Art.

Ashbery, John. "An Exhilarating Mess." *Newsweek*, February 23, 82-83.

Larson, Kay. "Sculpting Figuratively." *New York Magazine*, November 16, 120-23.

Morgan, Stuart. "Animal House: The Whitney Biennial." *Artscribe No. 21* (June).

Morris, Robert. "American Quartet." *Art in America* (December): 92-105.

1981 Biennial Exhibition. Exhibition catalogue. New York: Whitney Museum of American Art.

Schjeldahl, Peter. "The Hallelujah Trail." *The Village Voice*, March 18, 77.

Smith, Roberta. "Biennial Blues." *Art in America* (April): 92-101.

1980   Cohen, Ronny H. "Energism: An Attitude." *Artforum* (September): 16-23.

"Judith Shea at Willard." *Art in America* (October): 129-30.

Haskell, Barbara. "New Faces/ New Images." *Ocular* (Summer Quarter).

Larson, Kay. "For the First Time Women Are Leading, Not Following." *Art News* (October): 64-72.

Nadelman, Cynthia. "Fabric in Art." *Art News* (September): 244-47.

Raynor, Vivien. "Art: Two Women Take Crafts to Higher Plane." *New York Times*, June 27, C24.

Rickey, Carrie. "Of Crystal Palaces and Glass Houses." *The Village Voice*, April 14, 77.

Seven Artists. Exhibition catalogue. Purchase, New York: Neuberger Museum, State University of New York.

Silverthorne, Jeanne. "Judith Shea, Willard Gallery." *Artforum* (October): 81-82.

"Situation Esthetics: Impermanent Art and the Seventies Audience." *Artforum* (January): 22-29.

1979   Anderson, Alexandra. "Painting by the Yard." *Soho Weekly News,* June 28.

Askey, Ruth. "Clothing Constructions." *Artweek*, June 16, 7.

Connor, Maureen. "Form Follows Fashion." *Artforum* (December): 62-65.

Flood, Richard. "Philadelphia: 'Material Pleasures,' The Fabric Workshop at ICA." *Artforum* (October): 74-76.

Frank, Peter. "Museums on the Metroliner." *The Village Voice,* July 16, 64.

Material Pleasures. Exhibition catalogue. Philadelphia, Pennsylvania: Institute of Contemporary Art.

Muchnic, Suzanne. "Two Shows: From Trivial to Trenchant." *Los Angeles Times*, June 22, IV, 17.

Rickey, Carrie. "Art of Whole Cloth." *Art in America* (November): 72-83.

1977   Institute for Art and Urban Resources. "New Urban Landscapes: A Focus on Lower Manhattan." (Issue #9).

1976   *Rooms.* Exhibition catalogue. Long Island City, New York: P.S.1., The Institute for Art and Urban Resources.

Schwartz, Barbara. "New York: Sculpture and Craft." *Craft Horizons* (August): 49.

1975   Greenwood, Susan. "Artist Constructs Clothes that Allow Fabric to Flow." *Niagara Gazette,* August 24.

Endless Model, 1988 model for cast stone original
7' x 14" x 14"